How To Swim

Front Crawl

a step-by-step guide for beginners
learning front crawl technique

Mark Young

Author Online!

For more resources and swimming help visit
Mark Young's website at

www.swim-teach.com

Mark Young is a well-established swimming instructor with over twenty years experience of teaching thousands of adults and children to swim. He has taken nervous, frightened children and adults with a fear of water and made them happy and confident swimmers. He has also turned many of average ability into advanced swimmers. This book draws on his experiences and countless successes to put together this simplistic methodical approach to swimming.

Also by Mark Young

Step-By-Step Guides
How To Swim Breaststroke
How To Swim Backstroke
How To Swim Butterfly

How To Be A Swimming Teacher
The Definitive Guide to Becoming a
Successful Swimming Teacher

A Catalogue record for this book is available from the British Library

ISBN 9780992742836

Published by: Educate & Learn Publishing, Hertfordshire, UK

Graphics by Mark Young, courtesy of Poser V6.0

Design and typeset by Mark Young

Published in association with www.swim-teach.com

Contents

Page

How to use this book

Learning how to swim can be a frustrating experience sometimes, especially for an adult. Kick with your legs, pull with your arms, breathe in, and breathe out and do it all at the right time. Before you know it you've got a hundred and one things to think about and do all at the same time or in the right sequence.

How To Swim Front Crawl is designed to break down the stroke into its component parts, those parts being body position, legs, arms, breathing and timing and coordination. An exercise or series of exercises are then assigned to that part along with relevant teaching points and technique tips, to help focus only on that stroke part.

The exercises form a reference section for front crawl, complete with technique tips, teaching points and common mistakes for each individual exercise.

What exactly are these exercises?

Each specific exercise focuses on a certain part of the swimming stroke, for example the body position, the leg kick, the arms, the breathing or the timing and coordination, all separated into easy to learn stages. Each one contains a photograph of the exercise being performed, a graphical diagram and all the technique elements and key focus points that are relevant to that particular exercise.

How will they help?

They break down your swimming technique into its core elements and then force you to focus on that certain area. For example if you are performing a leg kick exercise, the leg kick is isolated and therefore your focus and concentration is only on the legs. The technical information and key focus points then fix your concentration on the most important elements of the leg kick. The result: a more efficient and technically correct leg kick. The same then goes for exercises for the arms, breathing, timing and coordination and so on.

Will they help to learn and improve your swimming strokes?

Yes, definitely! Although it is not the same as having a swimming teacher with you to correct you, these practical exercises perfectly compliment lessons or help to enhance your practice time in the pool. They not only isolate certain areas but also can highlight your bad habits. Once you've worked though each element of the stroke and practiced the exercises a few times, you will slowly eliminate your bad habits. The result: a more efficient and technically correct swimming stroke, swum with less effort!

Front Crawl

technique overview

Swimming with good front crawl technique is a desire that many long for. Whether its for competition, triathlon or just to feel and look good in your local pool, front crawl is the swimming stroke everyone wants to know how to swim well.

Front crawl is the fastest, most efficient stroke of them all. This is largely down to the streamlined body position and continuous propulsion from the arms and legs. The alternating action of the arms and legs is relatively easy on the joints and the stroke as a whole develops aerobic capacity faster than any other stroke. In competitive terms it is usually referred to as Freestyle.

The constant alternating arm action generates almost all of the propulsion and is the most efficient arm action of the four basic swimming strokes. The leg action promotes a horizontal, streamlined body position and balances the arm action but provides little propulsion.

Front crawl breathing technique requires the head to be turned so that the mouth clears the water but causes minimal upset to the balance of the body from its normal streamlined position.

The timing and coordination of the arms and legs occur most commonly with six leg kicks to one arm cycle. However, stroke timing can vary, with a four beat cycle and even a two beat cycle, which is most commonly used in long distance swims and endurance events.

Body Position

The overall body position for front crawl is as streamlined and as flat as possible at the water surface, with the head in-line with the body.

The waterline is around the natural hairline with eyes looking forward and down.

If the position of the head is raised it will cause the position of the hips and legs to lower which in turn will increase frontal resistance, causing the stroke to be inefficient and the breathing technique to be incorrect.

If the head position is too low it will cause the legs to rise and the kick to lose its efficiency.

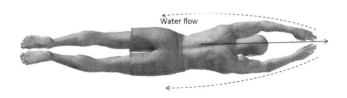

Streamlined body position minimises drag, allowing efficient movement through the water

Shoulders remain at the surface and roll with the arm action. Hips also roll with the stroke technique, close to the water surface and the legs remain in line with the body.

Common Body Position Mistakes

The common body position mistakes made are with head position and hand and feet position during the stroke.

If the head is too high over the water surface, it will cause the legs and feet to be lower under the water surface and cause the overall body position to be angled and therefore very inefficient.

Hands and feet must be together throughout the swimming stroke as this gives the body its streamlined efficiency, allowing it to move smoothly though the water.

If the hands or feet move apart it causes the overall shape of the body in the water to become wider and therefore inefficient.

The best exercise to practice perfecting the correct body position and shape is a push and glide from the poolside. The swimmer pushes off from the pool wall or floor and glides across the water surface, keeping the head central and hands and feet touching together.

Leg Kick

The leg kick for front crawl originates from the hips and both legs kick with equal force.

The legs kick in an up and down alternating action, with the propulsive phase coming from the down kick. There should be a slight bend in the knee due to the water pressure, in order to produce the propulsion required on the down kick.

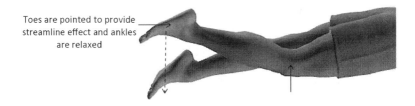

Toes are pointed to provide streamline effect and ankles are relaxed

Downward kick provides propulsion   Knee is relaxed and slightly bent

The downward kick begins at the hip and uses the thigh muscles to straighten the leg at the knee, ending with the foot extended to allow it's surface area to bear upon the water. As the leg moves upwards, the sole of the foot and the back of the leg press upwards and backwards against the water.

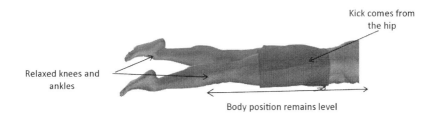

Kick comes from the hip

Relaxed knees and ankles

Body position remains level

The upward kick slows and stops as the leg nears and minimally breaks the water surface. Ankles are relaxed and toes pointed to give an in-toeing effect when kicking and the leg kick depth should be within the overall depth of the body.

Common Leg Kick Mistakes

It is very common to kick from the knees during front crawl, in an attempt to generate some propulsion and movement. This can also lead to a very stiff and robotic kicking action. The kick must originate from the hip and be a smooth movement with relaxed knee and ankle joints.

Another common mistake is to make the kicking movements too large. In other words, the feet come out over the water surface causing excessive splash and again wasting valuable energy.

A good exercise to practice the leg kick is holding a float or a kick board and kicking along the length of the pool with face down. This will allow the swimmer to focus purely on the leg kick, ensuring it is a relaxed and flowing up and down movement.

Arms

The continuous alternating arm action provides the majority of the power and propulsion of the entire swimming stroke.

entry

The hand enters the water at a 45 degree angle, finger tips first, thumb side down. The hand entry should be between shoulder and head line with a slight elbow bend.

catch

The hand reaches forward under the water without over stretching and the arm fully extends just under the water surface.

propulsive phase

The hand sweeps through the water downwards, inwards and then upwards. The elbow is high at the end of the down sweep and remains high throughout the in-sweep. The hand pulls through towards the thigh and upwards to the water surface.

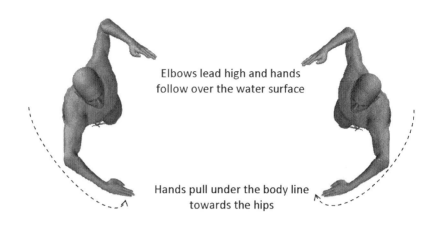

Elbows lead high and hands follow over the water surface

Hands pull under the body line towards the hips

recovery phase

The elbow bends to exit the water first. Hand and fingers fully exit the water and follow a straight path along the bodyline over the water surface. The elbow is bent and high and the arm is fully relaxed.

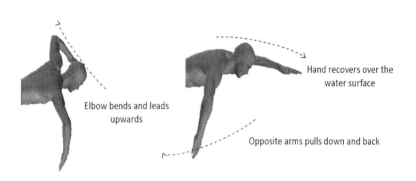

Elbow bends and leads upwards

Hand recovers over the water surface

Opposite arms pulls down and back

Common Arm Technique Mistakes

The arm action can bring about many mistakes, the most common being a deep propulsive phase and a very high recovery phase.

Both of these mistakes will disturb the body position, which will in turn create an inefficient overall swimming stroke. Both a deep arm pull and a high arm recovery over the water surface will also cause excessive body roll.

The best exercise for practicing and correcting these common mistakes is holding a float in one hand and swimming using single arm pulls. This will force the swimmer to focus on the arm technique whilst ensuring that the body position remains level and correct.

The head turns to the side on inhalation for front crawl breathing technique. The head begins to turn at the end of the upward arm sweep and turns enough for the mouth to clear the water and inhale. The head turns back into the water just as the arm recovers over and the hand returns to the water. Breathing can be bilateral (alternate sides every one and a half stroke cycles) or unilateral (same side) depending of the stroke cycle and distance to be swum.

Breath IN as the arm pulls through and the head turns to the side

Types of Breathing Technique

Trickle Breathing

The breath is slowly exhaled through the mouth and nose into the water during the propulsive phase of the arm pull. The exhalation is controlled to allow inhalation to take place easily as the arm recovers.

Explosive Breathing

The breath is held after inhalation during the propulsive arm phase and then released explosively, part in and part out of the water, as the head is turned to the side.

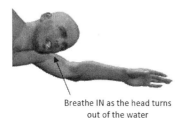

Breathe IN as the head turns out of the water

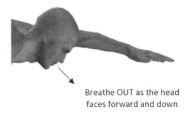

Breathe OUT as the head faces forward and down

Common Breathing Mistakes

It is very common, especially for beginners, to perform explosive breathing without knowing they are doing so. Holding the breath during the swimming stroke comes naturally to most people but it is not necessarily the most energy efficient way of swimming.

Breath holding causes an increase in carbon dioxide in the system, which increase the urgency to breathe. This can cause swimmers to become breathless very quickly.

Trickle breathing is the most effective breathing technique for beginners as it allows a gentle release of carbon dioxide from the lungs, which then makes inhalation easier.

Another common mistake is to lift the head instead of roll the head to the side. Lifting the head causes the legs to sink and the overall body position to be disturbed and the swimming stroke to be inefficient.

The best exercise for perfecting trickle breathing and ensuring the head is not lifting is to hold a float with a diagonal grip and kick. The diagonal grip allows space for the head to roll to the side.

Timing

The timing and coordination for front crawl usually occurs naturally.

The arms should provide a powerful propulsive alternating action whilst leg kicks also remain continuous and alternating.

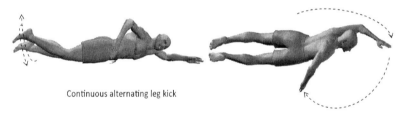

Continuous alternating leg kick

Continuous alternating arm action

However, there are a few variations.

Six beat cycle – each leg kicks three down kicks per arm cycle. The cycle is normally taught to beginners and used for sprint swims.
Four beat cycle – each leg kicks down twice for each arm pull.
Two-beat cycle – each leg kicks one downbeat per arm cycle. Long distance swimmers normally use this timing cycle, where the leg kick acts as a counter balance instead of a source of propulsion.

Common Mistakes

These various timing and coordination cycles bring varying degrees of mistakes, the most common being an attempt to kick too fast.

The required speed of the leg kick and therefore the timing cycle required for the stroke depends on the distance that is to be swum. A long distance swim requires the leg kick to counter balance the arm action, so the two beat cycle is best used. The short sprint requires a faster leg kick so the six beat cycle is needed so that the legs can provide more propulsion.

It is easy to kick with a fast leg kick and unknowingly allow the arm action to also speed up. This results in a loss of arm technique and overall body shape leading to a poor and inefficient swimming stroke.

Catch up is the best swimming exercise to not only establish correct timing and coordination cycle but to experiment with different timing cycles, as the delayed arm action slows down the exercise.

Front Crawl

exercises

FRONT CRAWL: Body Position

Holding the poolside

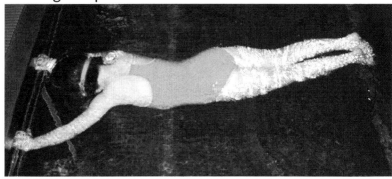

Aim: to encourage confidence in a floating position.

The swimmer holds the poolside for added security and some assistance may be required, as some people will not naturally float.

Hands holding the
poolside or rail

Overall body position is as horizontal as possible,
depending on the swimmers own buoyancy.

Key Actions
Relax
Keep the head tucked between the arms
Stretch out as far as you can
Keep your feet together

Technical Focus
Head is central and still
Face is submerged
Eyes are looking downwards
Shoulders should be level
Hips are close to the surface
Legs are together and in line with the body

Common Faults
Failure to submerge the face
Overall body is not relaxed
Head is not central
Whole body is not remaining straight
Feet are not together

FRONT CRAWL: Body Position

Static practice holding floats

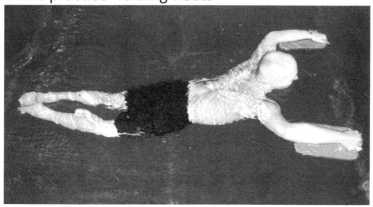

Aim: to help the swimmer develop confidence in their own buoyancy.

A float can be held under each arm or a single float held out in front, depending on levels of confidence and ability. Some swimmers may need extra assistance if they lack natural buoyancy.

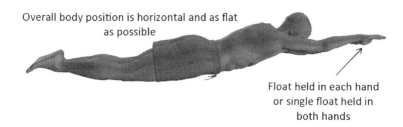

Overall body position is horizontal and as flat as possible

Float held in each hand or single float held in both hands

Key Actions
Relax
Keep the head tucked between the arms
Stretch out as far as you can
Keep your feet together

Technical Focus
Head is central and still
Face is submerged
Eyes are looking downwards
Shoulders should be level
Hips are close to the surface
Legs are together and in line with the body

Common Faults
Failure to submerge the face
Head is not central
Whole body is not remaining straight
Feet and hands are not together

FRONT CRAWL: Body Position

Push and glide from standing

 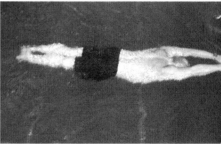

Aim: to develop correct body position and confidence in pushing off.

The swimmer can start with arms stretched out in front and pushes off from the pool floor or from the wall with one foot and glides through the water unaided.

Legs push off from
pool side or pool floor

Direction of travel

Key Actions
Push hard from the side/pool floor
Keep your head tucked between your arms
Stretch out as far as you can
Keep your hands together
Keep your feet together

Technical Focus
Initial push should be enough to gain good movement
Head remains still and central
Face submerged so that the water is at brow level
Shoulders should be level
Legs in line with the body

Common Faults
Failure to submerge the face
Push off is too weak
Whole body is not remaining straight
Feet are not together

FRONT CRAWL: Body Position

Push and glide from the side holding floats

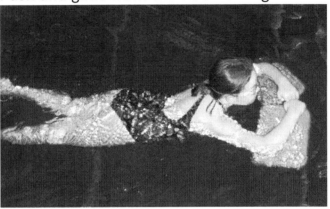

Aim: to develop correct body position whilst moving through the water.

Body position should be laying prone with the head up at this stage. The use of floats helps to build confidence, particularly in the weak or nervous swimmer. The floats create a slight resistance to the glide, but this is still a useful exercise.

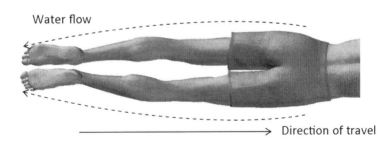

Water flow

Direction of travel

Key Actions

Push hard from the wall
Relax and float across the water
Keep your head still and look forward
Stretch out as far as you can
Keep your feet together

Technical Focus

Head remains still and central with the chin on the water surface
Eyes are looking forwards and downwards
Shoulders should be level and square
Hips are close to the surface
Legs are in line with the body

Common Faults

Push from the side is not hard enough
Head is not central
Whole body is not remaining straight
Feet are not together

FRONT CRAWL: Body Position

Push and glide from the poolside

Aim: to develop a streamlined body position whilst moving thorough the water.

Movement is created by pushing and gliding from holding position at the poolside.

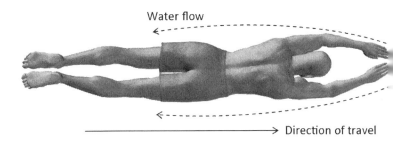

Water flow

Direction of travel

Streamlined body position minimises drag, allowing efficient movement through the water

Technical Focus

Head remains still and central
Face submerged so that the water is at brow level
Shoulders should be level and square
Legs are in line with the body
Overall body position should be streamlined

Key Actions

Push hard from the side
Stretch your arms out in front as you push
Keep your head tucked between your arms
Stretch out as far as you can
Keep your hands and feet together

Common Faults

Push off is too weak
Arms stretch in front after the push
Head is not central
Overall body position not in line
Hands or feet are not together

FRONT CRAWL: Legs

Sitting on the poolside kicking

Aim: to give the swimmer the feel of the water during the kick.

Sitting on poolside kicking is an ideal exercise for the beginner to practise correct leg kicking action with the added confidence of sitting on the poolside.

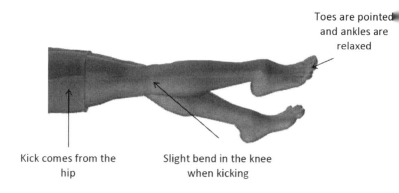

Toes are pointed and ankles are relaxed

Kick comes from the hip

Slight bend in the knee when kicking

Key Actions
Kick with straight legs
Pointed toes
Make a small splash with your toes
Kick with floppy feet
Kick continuously

Technical Focus
Kick is continuous and alternating
Knee is only slightly bent
Legs are close together when they kick
Ankles are relaxed and the toes are pointed

Common Faults
Knees bend too much
Kick comes from the knee
Stiff ankles

FRONT CRAWL: Legs

Holding the poolside

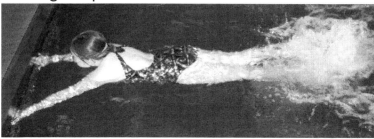

Aim: to encourage the swimmer to learn the kicking action.

Holding the poolside enhances confidence and helps develop leg strength and technique.

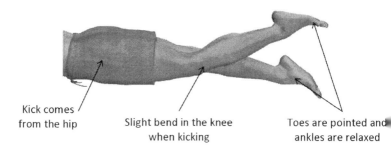

Kick comes from the hip

Slight bend in the knee when kicking

Toes are pointed and ankles are relaxed

Key Actions
Kick with straight legs
Pointed toes
Make a small splash with your toes
Kick with floppy feet
Kick from your hips
Kick continuously
Legs kick close together

Technical Focus
Kick comes from the hip
Kick is continuous and alternating
Knee is only slightly bent
Legs are close together when they kick
Ankles are relaxed and the toes are pointed
Kick should just break the water surface

Common Faults
Feet come out of the water
Kick comes from the knee
Legs are too deep in the water

FRONT CRAWL: Legs

Legs kick with a float held under each arm

Aim: to learn correct kicking technique and develop leg strength.

The added stability of two floats will help boost confidence in the weak swimmer.

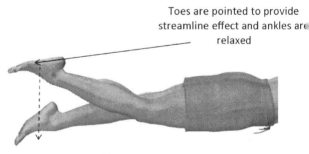

Toes are pointed to provide streamline effect and ankles are relaxed

Downward kick provides propulsion

Key Actions
Kick with straight legs
Pointed toes
Kick with floppy feet
Kick from your hips
Kick continuously

Technical Focus
Kick comes from the hip
Kick is continuous and alternating
Chin remains on the water surface
Legs are close together when they kick
Ankles are relaxed and the toes are pointed
Kick should just break the water surface
Upper body and arms should be relaxed

Common Faults
Head lifts above the surface, causing the legs to sink
Kick comes from the knee causing excessive bend
Kick is not deep enough
Legs are too deep in the water

FRONT CRAWL: Legs

Float held with both hands

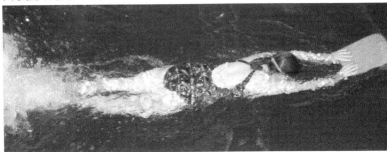

Aim: to practise and learn correct kicking technique.

Holding a float or kickboard out in front isolates the legs, encourages correct body position and develops leg strength.

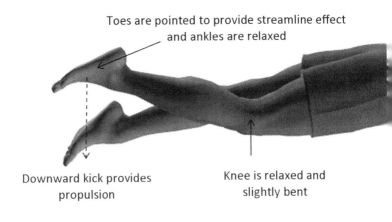

Toes are pointed to provide streamline effect and ankles are relaxed

Downward kick provides propulsion

Knee is relaxed and slightly bent

Key Actions
Kick with pointed toes
Make a small splash with your toes
Kick with floppy feet
Legs kick close together

Technical Focus
Kick comes from the hip
Kick is continuous and alternating.
Legs are close together when they kick
Ankles are relaxed and the toes are pointed.
Kick should just break the water surface.

Common Faults
Knees bend too much
Feet come out of the water
Kick comes from the knee
Legs are too deep in the water

FRONT CRAWL: Legs

Push and glide with added leg kick

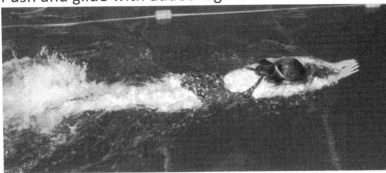

Aim: to develop correct body position and leg kick whilst holding the breath.

Push and glide without a float and add a leg kick whilst maintaining a streamlined body position.

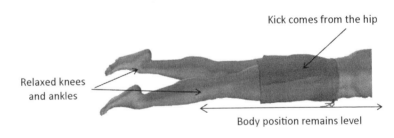

Kick comes from the hip

Relaxed knees
and ankles

Body position remains level

Key Actions
Kick with straight legs and pointed toes
Kick with floppy feet
Kick from your hips
Kick continuously

Technical Focus
Kick comes from the hip
Streamlined body position is maintained
Kick is continuous and alternating
Legs are close together when they kick
Ankles are relaxed and the toes are pointed
Kick should just break the water surface

Common Faults
Feet come out of the water
Stiff ankles
Kick is not deep enough
Legs are too deep in the water

FRONT CRAWL: Legs

Leg kick whilst holding a float vertically in front

Aim: to create resistance and help develop strength and stamina.

Holding a float vertically in front increases the intensity of the kicking action, which in turn develops leg strength and stamina.

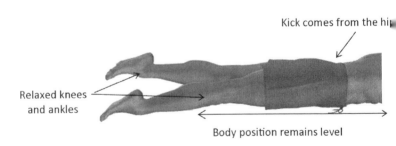

Kick comes from the hip

Relaxed knees and ankles

Body position remains level

Key Actions
Kick with straight legs and pointed toes
Kick with floppy feet
Kick from your hips
Kick continuously

Technical Focus
Kick comes from the hip
Streamlined body position is maintained
Kick is continuous and alternating
Legs are close together when they kick
Ankles are relaxed and the toes are pointed
Kick should just break the water surface

Common Faults
Feet come out of the water
Stiff ankles
Kick is not deep enough
Legs are too deep in the water

FRONT CRAWL: Arms

Standing on the poolside or in shallow water

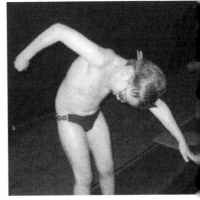

Aim: to practise correct arm movement whilst in a static position.

This is an exercise for beginners that can be practised on the poolside or standing in shallow water.

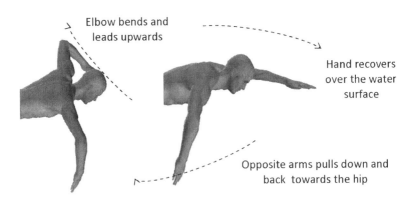

Elbow bends and leads upwards

Hand recovers over the water surface

Opposite arms pulls down and back towards the hip

Key Actions
Keep your fingers together
Continuous smooth action
Brush your hand past your thigh
Gradually bend your elbow

Technical Focus
Fingers should be together
Pull through to the hips
Elbow bends and leads upwards

Common Faults
Fingers are too wide apart
Pull is short and not to the thigh
Arms are too straight as they pull
Arms are too straight on recovery
Hand entry is wide of the shoulder line

FRONT CRAWL: Arms

Single arm practice with float held in one hand

Aim: to practise and improve correct arm technique

This practice allows the swimmer to develop arm technique whilst maintaining body position and leg kick. Holding a float with one hand gives the weaker swimmer security and allows the competent swimmer to focus on a single arm.

Elbow leads out of the water first

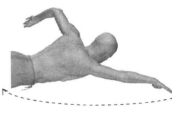

Arm pulls back through the water towards the hip

Key Actions

Keep your fingers together
Brush your hand past your thigh
Pull fast under the water
Make an 'S' shape under the water
Elbow out first
Reach over the water surface

Technical Focus

Fingertips enter first with thumb side down
Fingers should be together
Pull should be an elongated 'S' shape
Pull through to the hips
Elbow exits the water first
Fingers clear the water on recovery

Common Faults

Fingers are apart
Pull is short and not to the thigh
Lack of power in the pull
Arm pull is too deep underwater
Arms are too straight on recovery

FRONT CRAWL: Arms

Alternating arm pull whilst holding a float out in front

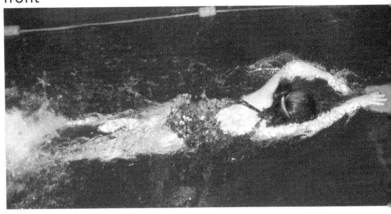

Aim: to develop coordination and correct arm pull technique.

The swimmer uses an alternating arm action. This also introduces a timing aspect, as the leg kick has to be continuous at the same time.

Arm pulls through towards the hip

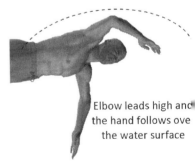

Elbow leads high and the hand follows over the water surface

Key Actions
Finger tips in first
Brush your hand past your thigh
Pull fast under the water
Elbow out first
Reach over the water surface

Technical Focus
Clean entry with fingertips first and thumb side down
Fingers should be together
Each arm pulls through to the hips
Elbow leads out first
Fingers clear the water on recovery

Common Faults
Fingers are too wide apart
Pull is short and not to the thigh
Lack of power in the pull
Arms are too straight on recovery
Hand entry is wide of shoulder line

FRONT CRAWL: Arms

Arm action using a pull-buoy

Aim: to develop arm pull strength, technique and coordination.

This is a more advanced exercise, which requires stamina and a degree of breathing technique.

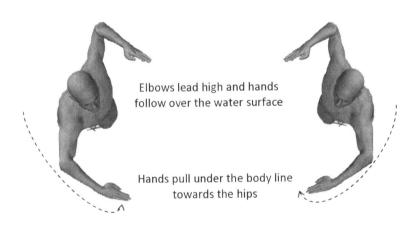

Elbows lead high and hands follow over the water surface

Hands pull under the body line towards the hips

Key Actions
Long strokes
Smooth continuous action
Brush your hand past your thigh
Make an 'S' shape under the water
Elbow out first
Reach over the water surface

Technical Focus
Fingertips enter first with thumb side down
Fingers should be together
Pull should be an elongated 'S' shape
Pull through to the hips
Elbow comes out first
Fingers clear the water on recovery

Common Faults
Pull is short and not to the thigh
Lack of power in the pull
Arms pull too deep under water
Arms are too straight on recovery
Hand entry is across the centre line

FRONT CRAWL: Arms

Push and glide adding arm cycles

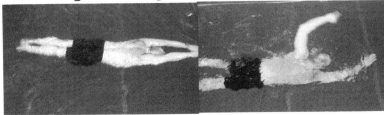

Aim: to combine correct arm action with a streamlined body position.

The swimmer performs a push and glide to establish body position and then adds arm cycles, whilst maintaining body position.

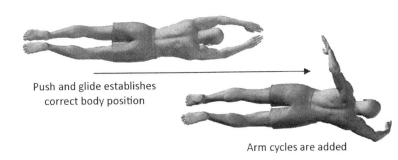

Push and glide establishes correct body position

Arm cycles are added

Key Actions

Finger tips in the water first
Brush your hand past your thigh
Make an 'S' shape under the water
Elbow out first
Reach over the water surface

Technical Focus

Clean entry with fingertips first
Pull should be an elongated 'S' shape
Pull through to the hips
Elbow comes out first
Fingers clear the water on recovery

Common Faults

Pull is short and not to the thigh
Lack of power in the pull
Arms are too straight under water
Arms are too straight on recovery
Hand entry is across centre line

FRONT CRAWL: Breathing

Standing and holding the poolside

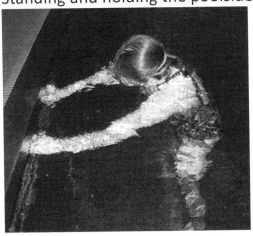

Aim: to practice and develop breathing technique.
The pupil stands and holds the pool rail with one arm extended, breathing to one side to introduce the beginner to breathing whilst having his/her face submerged.

BREATHE IN

Head turns to the side and mouth clears the water surface

BREATHE OUT

Head faces forward and down

Key Actions

Breathe out through your mouth
Blow out slowly and gently
Turn your head to the side when you breathe in
See how long you can make the breath last

Technical Focus

Breathing should be from the mouth
Breathing in should be when the head is turned to the side
Breathing out should be when the face is down

Common Faults

Breathing through the nose
Holding the breath

FRONT CRAWL: Breathing

Holding a float in front with diagonal grip

Aim: to encourage correct breathing technique whilst kicking.

The float is held in front; one arm extended fully, the other holding the near corner with elbow low. This creates a gap for the head and mouth to be turned in at the point of breathing.

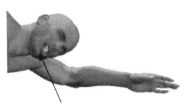

Breathe IN as the head turns out of the water

Breathe OUT as the head faces forward and down

Key Actions

Turn head towards the bent arm to breathe
Breathe out through your mouth
Blow out slowly and gently
Return head to the centre soon after breathing

Technical Focus

Breathing should be from the mouth
Breathing in should be when the head is turned to the side
Breathing out should be slow and controlled

Common Faults

Breathing through the nose
Holding the breath
Lifting the head and looking forward when breathing
Turning towards the straight arm

FRONT CRAWL: Breathing

Float held in one hand, arm action with breathing

Aim: to develop correct breathing technique whilst pulling with one arm.

This allows the swimmer to add the arm action to the breathing technique and perfect the timing of the two movements. The float provides support and keeps the exercise as a simple single arm practice.

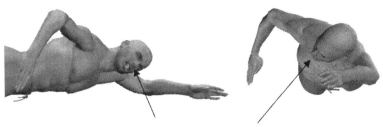

Breath IN as the arm pulls through and the head turns to the side

Key Actions
Turn head to the side of the pulling arm
Breathe out through your mouth
Blow out slowly and gently
Return head to the centre soon after breathing

Technical Focus
Head moves enough for mouth to clear the water
Breathing in occurs when the head is turned to the side
Breathing out should be slow
Breathing should be from the mouth

Common Faults
Turning towards the straight arm
Turning the head too much
Breathing through the nose
Holding the breath
Lifting the head and looking forward when breathing

FRONT CRAWL: Breathing

Float held in both hands, alternate arm pull with breathing

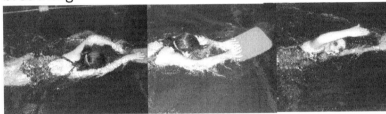

Aim: to practise bi-lateral breathing with the support of a float held out in front.

A single float is held in both hands and one arm pull is performed at a time with the head turning to breathe with each arm pull. Different arm action and breathing cycles can be used, for example; breathe every other arm pull or every three arm pulls.

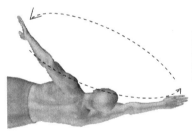

Head turns to the left side as the left arm pulls through and begins to recover

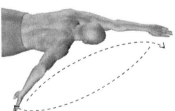

Head turns to the right side as the right arm pulls through and begins to recover

Key Actions

Keep head still until you need to breathe
Breathe every 3 strokes (or another pattern you may choose)
Turn head to the side as your arm pulls back
Return head to the centre soon after breathing
Breathe out through your mouth

Technical Focus

Head should be still when not taking a breath
Head movement should be minimal enough for mouth to clear
the water
Breathing in should be when the head is turned to the side
Breathing should be from the mouth

Common Faults

Turning towards the straight arm
Turning the head too much
Turning the head too early or late to breath
Lifting the head and looking forward when breathing

FRONT CRAWL: Timing

Front crawl catch up

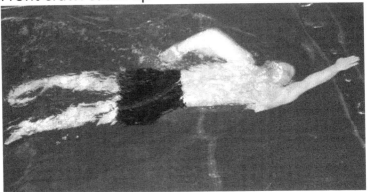

Aim: to practice correct stroke timing and develop coordination.

The opposite arm remains stationary until the arm performing the pull recovers to its starting position. This is an advanced exercise and encourages the swimmer to maintain body position and leg kick whilst practicing arm cycles.

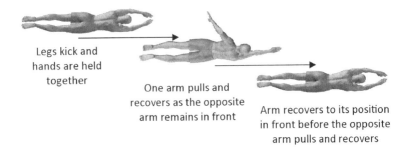

Legs kick and hands are held together

One arm pulls and recovers as the opposite arm remains in front

Arm recovers to its position in front before the opposite arm pulls and recovers

Key Actions

Finger tips in the water first
Brush your hand past your thigh
Make an 'S' shape under the water
Elbow out first
Reach over the water surface

Technical Focus

Clean entry with fingertips first
Pull should be an elongated 'S' shape
Pull through to the hips
Elbow comes out first
Fingers clear the water on recovery

Common Faults

One leg kick per arm pull ('one beat cycle')
Continuous leg kick but not enough arm pulls
Arm pull is too irregular

FRONT CRAWL
Full stroke

Aim: full stroke Front Crawl demonstrating correct leg action, arm action, breathing and timing.

Key Actions
Keep your head still until you breathe
Kick continuously from your hips
Stretch forward with each arm action
Pull continuously under your body
Count 3 leg kicks with each arm pull

Technical Focus
Stroke is smooth and continuous
Head in line with the body
Legs in line with the body
Head remains still
Leg kick is continuous and alternating
Arm action is continuous and alternating
Breathing is regular and to the side
Stroke ideally has a 6 beat cycle

Common Faults
Head moves from side to side
Legs kick from the knee
Leg action is too slow
Arm action is untidy and splashing
Excessive head movement when breathing o Head is lifted,
    causing legs to sink
Stroke is erratic and rushed

Front Crawl

common questions

When I swim front crawl I have to hold my breath, because my head does not come out of the water enough for me to catch any air. What am I doing wrong?

Firstly the fact that you are holding your breath in the first place can sometimes cause problems. If you hold your breath you have only a split second to breathe out and then in again, which can be very difficult. So much so that pupils I have taught in the past turn their head as if to breathe but continue to hold their breath.

It could be that your mouth is clearing the water enough to breathe but you are involuntarily continuing to hold your breath.

To overcome this you must breathe out into the water whilst swimming and then when you turn your head to breathe, you only have to breathe in. This makes breathing easier and more relaxed.

If as you suspect the problem is your head not clearing the water surface enough then we need to look at the basics of the breathing technique.

Firstly front crawl breathing technique involves rolling the head to one side and not lifting the head to face forward. Lifting your head upwards will result in that sinking feeling and your mouth will almost certainly not clear the water enough to breathe in.

Ensure that at the point where you roll your head to the side to breathe, your arm on that side must have pulled back to clear a space for your head to turn into. You must then breathe in just as your arm recovers over the water surface.

To ensure that your head rolls to the side enough try looking at your shoulder as you do it. This will ensure you are actually rolling your head and not lifting it. It will also help your mouth to clear to water so that you can breathe.

If you are still struggling try to exaggerate your movement by rolling your head to look at ceiling above you. Your arm recovery will have to be very high in order to achieve this but it will almost certainly allow you to breathe. However, this is of course technically incorrect but the exaggerated movement will allow you to practice the movement and become confident with breathing. It is therefore important to readjust the technique once you have become proficient by rolling the head the minimum amount so as not to disturb your overall body position.

How do I coordinate the arms and legs for front crawl? I am just learning to swim and when swimming my arms my legs will not move in time with each other.

The problem you are referring to is related to your coordination.

Front crawl is an alternating stroke. In other words as one arm pulls the other recovers and as one leg kicks downwards the other kicks upwards.

Unlike breaststroke which is a simultaneous swimming stroke where both arms pull at the same time and both legs also kick at the same time.

You will find that your coordination will favour one more than the other because one will come more naturally than the other.

The timing and coordination of front crawl arms and legs is not something that comes naturally to some people but there is no reason why it cannot be learnt.

A simple exercise to try out is front crawl 'catch up'. Hold a float or kick board with both hands and kick your legs. Then perform one arm pull at a time, taking hold of the float after each complete arm action. You are therefore performing front crawl arms one at a time whilst attempting to maintain your leg kick. Holding the float will help you to focus on your leg kick whilst using your arms.

As for how fast to kick your legs, there is no right or wrong here. The 6 beat cycle is the most traditional where there are 6 leg kicks to each arm cycle (there are 2 arm pulls to a cycle). A 4 beat cycle is also a common pattern and a 1 beat cycle is one of the most common.

Keep in mind that most of the power to generate the movement for front crawl comes from the arms and the legs are there mainly to balance or provide a small amount of power.

For this reason a 2 beat cycle can be quite effective especially as kicking the legs at faster speeds can be very tiring. One leg kicks and one arm pulls.

What you have described is very common and with some practice you will soon have a respectful front crawl swimming stroke.

I seem to lose my front crawl technique and my kicking when I get tired. The first few lengths are ok but after that when I get tired it's all gone.

Losing your technique because of tiredness is very common and as front crawl is high energy consuming swimming stroke, it doesn't take long before it all falls apart.

A couple of things to think about that might help you out.

Firstly you mentioned your kicking. Be mindful of how much kicking you are actually doing. It is very common to kick far more than you really need to, especially over a long distance.

Remember the power and propulsion for front crawl comes mainly from the arm action. Propulsion is generated from the leg kick but no way near as much as from the arms.

Watch a long distance front crawl swimmer, for example a triathlete. Each leg kicks once for every arm pull, serving less as propulsion and more as a counter balance to the arm actions, to help keep the stroke as whole balanced and even.

On the other hand take a short distance front crawl sprint, over 50 or 100 meters. The legs kick with enormous speed and power to provide maximum propulsion and assistance to the arms with this short distance using up all energy.

Conclusion: less leg kicks equals energy saved - energy that you will need in order to swim a longer distance.

Secondly be mindful of your breathing and in particular how often you breathe. Assuming that you exhale into the water (the easiest and most natural method) and not hold your breath, which only serves to make you more tired.

Once again the distance being swum will dictate the frequency that you need to breathe. Longer distances more often and shorter distances less. This may sound obvious but it is all too easy to set off from the start and get the pace and frequency of the breathing wrong, despite what might feel right at the time, only for it to catch you out later in the swim.

Breathing every stroke or every other stroke will help to keep a steady pace and hopefully allow you to last longer. Bilateral breathing (alternating the side you breathe to by taking a breath every three arm pulls) is a nice even and steady breathing pattern. However even this cannot be maintained over long distances. Taking a breath every stroke cycle will cover longer distances, which again you will see if you watch any long distance swimmer.

Lastly there is the age-old problem of fitness. Your fitness and stamina will ultimately dictate how far you can swim before your body tells you it has had enough. Like any form of exercise, the more you do it the fitter and stronger you become.

"Now that you have finished my book, would you please consider writing a review? Reviews are the best way readers discover great new books. I would truly appreciate it."

Mark Young

For more information about learning to swim and improving your swimming strokes and swimming technique visit:

swim-teach.com

"The number one resource for learning to swim and improving swimming technique."

www.swim-teach.com

Printed in Great Britain
by Amazon